COLLECTION EDITOR: **JENNIFER GRÜNWALD**
ASSISTANT EDITOR: **CAITLIN O'CONNELL**
ASSOCIATE MANAGING EDITOR: **KATERI WOODY**
EDITOR, SPECIAL PROJECTS: **MARK D. BEAZLEY**
VP PRODUCTION & SPECIAL PROJECTS: **JEFF YOUNGQUIST**
SVP PRINT, SALES & MARKETING: **DAVID GABRIEL**
BOOK DESIGN: **JEFF POWELL**

EDITOR IN CHIEF: **C.B. CEBULSKI**
CHIEF CREATIVE OFFICER: **JOE QUESADA**
PRESIDENT: **DAN BUCKLEY**
EXECUTIVE PRODUCER: **ALAN FINE**

WOLVERINE: SAVAGE ORIGINS. Contains material originally published in magazine form as WOLVERINE: SEASON ONE and WOLVERINE #20. First printing 2018. ISBN 978-0-7851-6673-3. Published by MARVEL WORLDWIDE, INC., a subsidiary of MARVEL ENTERTAINMENT, LLC. OFFICE OF PUBLICATION: 135 West 50th Street, New York, NY 10020. Copyright © 2018 MARVEL No similarity between any of the names, characters, persons, and/or institutions in this magazine with those of any living or dead person or institution is intended, and any such similarity which may exist is purely coincidental. **Printed in Canada.** DAN BUCKLEY, President, Marvel Entertainment; JOHN NEE, Publisher; JOE QUESADA, Chief Creative Officer; TOM BREVOORT, SVP of Publishing; DAVID BOGART, SVP of Business Affairs & Operations, Publishing & Partnership; DAVID GABRIEL, SVP of Sales & Marketing, Publishing; JEFF YOUNGQUIST, VP of Production & Special Projects; DAN CARR, Executive Director of Publishing Technology; ALEX MORALES, Director of Publishing Operations; DAN EDINGTON, Managing Editor; SUSAN CRESPI, Production Manager; STAN LEE, Chairman Emeritus. For information regarding advertising in Marvel Comics or on Marvel.com, please contact Vit DeBellis, Custom Solutions & Integrated Advertising Manager, at vdebellis@marvel.com. For Marvel subscription inquiries, please call 888-511-5480. **Manufactured between 4/27/2018 and 5/29/2018 by SOLISCO PRINTERS, SCOTT, QC, CANADA.**

10 9 8 7 6 5 4 3 2 1

WOLVERINE

WRITERS
BEN ACKER
& BEN BLACKER

ARTIST
SALVA ESPIN
WITH
CAM SMITH

COLOR ARTIST
JIM CHARALAMPIDIS

LETTERER
VC'S JOE CARAMAGNA

COVER ARTIST
JULIAN TOTINO TEDESCO

EDITOR
JORDAN D. WHITE

EXECUTIVE EDITOR
TOM BREVOORT

SAVAGE ORIGINS

WHILE I TENDED TO OUR GUEST, JAMES RETURNED TO WORK AT DEPARTMENT H, A DIVISION OF THE CANADIAN DEPARTMENT OF NATIONAL DEFENSE.

HE SAID HE'D SUBTLY POKE AROUND WITH OUR COLLEAGUES, TO SEE IF HE COULD FIND OUT IF ANYONE KNEW ANYTHING ABOUT WOLVERINE.

BUT SUBTLETY WAS NEVER JAMES' STRONG SUIT.

SKA-FING!

IT'S NOT SUCH A STRANGE IDEA, GRAFTING A METAL COATING TO HUMAN BONE. I HEARD A STORY ABOUT THAT ONCE.

EXCELLENT! THE EXO-SUIT IS FULLY RESISTANT! YOU SHOULD BE ABLE TO TRY PILOTING IT IN--

WHAT STORY? FROM SOMEONE IN HERE?

AH, YOU KNOW HOW IT GOES, HUDSON. A PLACE LIKE THIS--A GOVERNMENT FACILITY WHERE DEFENSE TESTING GETS DONE? ALL KINDS OF PULP STORIES ARISE OVER THE YEARS.

THERE'S A LURID ONE I HEARD ABOUT A SECRET PROJECT A WHILE BACK THAT NEARLY CLOSED DOWN DEPARTMENT H. SOME SORT OF HUMAN TESTING, WHEREBY ADAMANTIUM WAS GRAFTED TO THE SUBJECT'S SKELETON. FROM WHAT I'VE HEARD, THE SUBJECT WAS PARTICULARLY SUITED TO THE EXPERIMENTS.

WHAT HAPPENED TO THE SUBJECT?

THAT'S THE SICK PART. APPARENTLY HE BROKE HIS PROGRAMMING, SLAUGHTERED EVERYONE HERE, AND NEARLY BURNED THE PLACE TO ASH. THEN "SUBJECT X" DISAPPEARED INTO THE WOODS.

HE'S... DANGEROUS?

IF HE EXISTS, JAMES. IF HE EXISTS, THEN YES. HE'S VERY DANGEROUS.

GRAR!

HUNF.

LIVING IN THE WOODS AS AN ANIMAL...HAD HE TRULY LOST ALL HUMANITY? LANGUAGE? EMPATHY?

I'M GOING TO SING TO YOU, OKAY? DON'T FREAK OUT. MY VOICE ISN'T GREAT.

♪ LET US FLY, SAID THE LADY, I FEAR WE SHALL BE SLAIN... ♪

♪ ...TAKE MY HAND, SAID THE SOLDIER, AND NEVER FEAR AGAIN. FA LA LA LA, FA LA LA LA... ♪

♪ ...THEN HE PULLED OUT SWORD AND PISTOL, AND CAUSED THEM TO RATTLE... ♪

OKAY... 'SOKAY...

SHHH... JUST REST... REST...

...I DON'T THINK SO, JAMES. HE TALKED. HE'S STILL A PERSON, EVEN IF THOSE CLAWS WERE--

--HE'S WAKING UP. I'LL SEE YOU SOON.

YOU ?COUGH?... DID YOU...SING TO ME?

MY NAME IS HEATHER HUDSON. MY HUSBAND JAMES AND I FOUND YOU. THIS IS OUR CABIN.

HE THINKS YOU'RE DANGEROUS. ARE YOU?

I... I DON'T KNOW.

DO YOU REMEMBER ANYTHING? WHO YOU ARE? HOW LONG YOU WERE IN THE WOODS? WHAT HAPPENED TO YOU BEFORE?

NO. NOTHING.

BUT IF YOUR HUSBAND THINKS I MIGHT BE DANGEROUS...THEN MAYBE HE KNOWS SOMETHING ABOUT WHO I AM.

"A NEARLY PERFECT WEAPON WAS HUMANELY CREATED FROM A *MUTANT* WHO VOLUNTEERED FOR THE PROGRAM. YOU KNOW WHAT A MUTANT IS, JAMES?"

"A HUMAN WHO POSSESSES A GENETIC TRAIT CALLED AN X-GENE THAT ALLOWS HIM TO DEVELOP ULTRA-HUMAN ABILITIES."

"A+. AND THIS VOLUNTEER'S MUTATION GAVE HIM A RAPID HEALING FACTOR. HE WAS THE PERFECT CANDIDATE."

"SO WHAT HAPPENED?"

"NOTHING 'HAPPENED.'"

"THE PROJECT WAS DISCONTINUED DUE TO BUDGETARY SHUT-DOWNS."

OH GOD! I'M SORRY, I-- I DIDN'T KNOW IT WAS YOU.

I'M GONNA GO. I AIN'T A HOUSE PET. YOU'RE LIABLE TO GET SCRATCHED IF I STAY.

IT SOUNDS TO ME LIKE YOU'RE MAKING THE VERY HUMAN CHOICE TO LEAVE. WHICH MEANS YOU CAN PROBABLY CONTROL YOUR ANIMAL IMPULSES.

NO!

YOU CAN'T CONTROL THE ANIMAL!

EXCUSE ME?!

OOH, PEARLS.

PUM-FAK!

SNIK! SNAK! SNIK! SNAK!

KAFF!

URK!

HELP! HEATHER?

CRAP.

RAAAARGH!

SHINK!

KZKK!

YOU'RE MISSING IT. NOW HE'S KILLING THE HELICOPTER.

GRAARGH!

HEATHER IS RIGHT THERE! THERE'S EVERY CHANCE HE'LL KILL HER NEXT! I'M NOT GOING TO STAND HERE DRINKING TEA! I'M GOING IN!

THE GUARDIAN ARMOR COULD USE A FIELD TEST...

I GOT THIS.

YOU'RE KIDDING ME. DON'T GO TOWARDS THE INSANE RAMPAGING MAN AND HIS AMAZING UNBREAKABLE CLAWS!

Camera 01

WE'RE REESTABLISHING THE WEAPON X PROGRAM.

WE WILL SEEK TO REPLICATE AND IMPROVE UPON THE U.S. SUPER-SOLDIER SERUM, WHICH SPAWNED CAPTAIN AMERICA, TO CREATE AN UNSTOPPABLE CANADIAN GUARDIAN.

DR. HADDOCK, HUMAN TESTING--

WHAT'LL MAKE THIS SERUM DIFFERENT? HOW WILL IT SUSTAIN?

YOU CAN'T BE BUYING INTO THIS, FRED. OUR ARMOR WORKS! WE SAW IT--

WEAPON X WILL RUN *PARALLEL* TO THE GUARDIAN WEAPONRY PROGRAM, DR. HUDSON.

THE HEALING FACTOR IN LOGAN'S GENETIC MATERIAL WILL COMBINE WITH GAMMA-IRRADIATED DNA FROM THE HULK WITHOUT BREAKING DOWN. THAT WILL PROVIDE THE FOUNDATION FOR THE SERUM.

HOW-- HOW WILL YOU GET HULK DNA?

YEAH, I DON'T KNOW WHO YOU ARE.

YOU DON'T REMEMBER ME? HURTS.

STILL, I'LL TAKE CARE OF THIS WENDIGO OP FOR YOU, BUDDY. FOR OLD TIMES' SAKE.

YOU *KNOW* ME? YOU KNOW WHO I *AM?* WHO I *WAS?*

WHO AM I?!

WHY AM I DOING THIS?

IS IT TO STOP JAMES? OR TO PROTECT LOGAN?

THE OUTCOME IS THE SAME, I KNOW. BUT THE REASON MATTERS.

JAMES SAID GOODBYE TO ME AND TOLD ME HIS MISSION. IT'S NOT ABOUT WENDIGO. HE'S TO BRING BACK WOLVERINE, DEAD OR ALIVE. I KNOW JAMES THINKS HE'S DOING GOOD, BUT SOMETIMES HE'S BLINDED BY HIS PATRIOTISM.

THAT PATRIOTISM COULD GET LOGAN KILLED.

AND DR. HADDOCK'S DECISION TO TEAM JAMES WITH THIS VICTOR CREED PERSON...I DON'T KNOW WHO HE IS, BUT HE CLEARLY HAS IT IN FOR LOGAN.

TRACKED THEM THROUGH JAMES' ARMOR. ONLY HOPE I'VE ARRIVED BEFORE LOGAN GETS--

SKA-BOOM!

HEY!

I MISSED YOU ON PURPOSE! STILL!

TELL YOU WHAT, YOU TWO WORK OUT YOUR MARRIAGE ISSUES, AND I'LL GO BEAT UP THE BAD GUY.

OUR MARRIAGE IS FINE!

YOU'RE THE BAD GUY, LOGAN!

PUT ME DOWN!

I'M TAKING YOU TO SAFETY SO I CAN FINISH THIS MISSION.

WHY? SO HADDOCK GIVES YOU A GOLD STAR?

BUT... BUT THAT... WE DON'T HAVE TIME FOR THIS...

BLAM!

SO WOLVERINE IS SAFELY BEHIND BARS AT DEPARTMENT H! HE'S AN ANIMAL, HEATHER. DOESN'T THE FACT THAT HE ESCAPED THE FACILITY PROVE THAT TO YOU?

I LET HIM ESCAPE.

WHAT?!

AND DOESN'T THE FACT THAT HE RAN OFF TO SAVE WENDIGO PROVE ANYTHING TO *YOU?*

"THE ENTIRE ENDEAVOR WAS HUBRIS, R. HADDOCK."

WOLVERINE FOUND HIS HUMANITY AND STILL DEFEATED CREED, A MONSTER WHO TRIED TO KILL ALL OF US.

NONETHELESS, THE WEAPON X INITIATIVE WILL REMAIN OPEN.

HOW MANY PEOPLE HAVE TO DIE? WHAT WE PROPOSE ACHIEVES THE SAME GOALS, DOCTOR, WITHOUT ENDANGERING LIVES OR EXPERIMENTING UNNECESSARILY.

IT'LL BE CANADA'S ANSWER TO THE AVENGERS. BUT WITH... AN ADDITIONAL ANGLE.

I LIKE TO THINK THAT TIME CHANGED LOGAN TOO.

HE MAY NOT KNOW WHERE HE CAME FROM OR WHERE HE'S GOING, BUT IT SEEMS HE'LL BE OKAY WITH THE JOURNEY.

YOU'RE THE APPOINTMENT HEATHER SET ME UP WITH? WHAT'RE YOU, A SHRINK?

NOT EXACTLY, LOGAN, NO.

WHAT THEN? SHE SAID YOU COULD HELP ME WITH MY PAST.

YOUR PAST. YOUR PRESENT. EVEN YOUR FUTURE. I CAN HELP WITH ALL OF IT.

THIS SOME SORTA CULT THING?

NOTHING LIKE THAT. I'M A MUTANT, LIKE YOU. A TELEPATH.

YOU CAN READ MY MIND?

I CAN TRY. FROM WHAT I'VE HEARD, IT WON'T BE EASY. BUT I ASK ONE THING OF YOU IN RETURN. I RUN A SCHOOL. A SCHOOL FOR MUTANTS.

I'M TOO OLD FOR SCHOOLIN'.

IT'S ALSO... MORE THAN A SCHOOL. IF YOU'LL JOIN US, I CAN NOT ONLY ASSIST YOU TO RECALL YOUR PAST BUT HELP YOU TAME THE FUTURE.

"TAME," HUH? LIKE KEEPIN' THE ANIMAL AT BAY?

YOU'VE PROVEN THAT NOT ONLY IS THAT YOUR DESIRE BUT THAT YOU ARE CAPABLE OF DOING IT WHEN SURROUNDED BY FRIENDS.

DON'T REMEMBER EVER JOININ' ANYTHING ON PURPOSE BEFORE, BUT WHO'S TO SAY IT NEVER HAPPENED?

OKAY. I'M IN. BUT DON'T GET SORE IF I START SCRATCHIN' UP YOUR FURNITURE.

OH, YOU'LL FIT IN JUST FINE. I CAN TELL.

UH-HUH. I'LL BELIEVE IT WHEN I SEE IT. BUT I'M GLAD TO GET THE SHOT.

YOU'RE WELCOME, LOGAN.

THAT WASN'T A THANK YOU.

I'M SURE IT WASN'T.

End

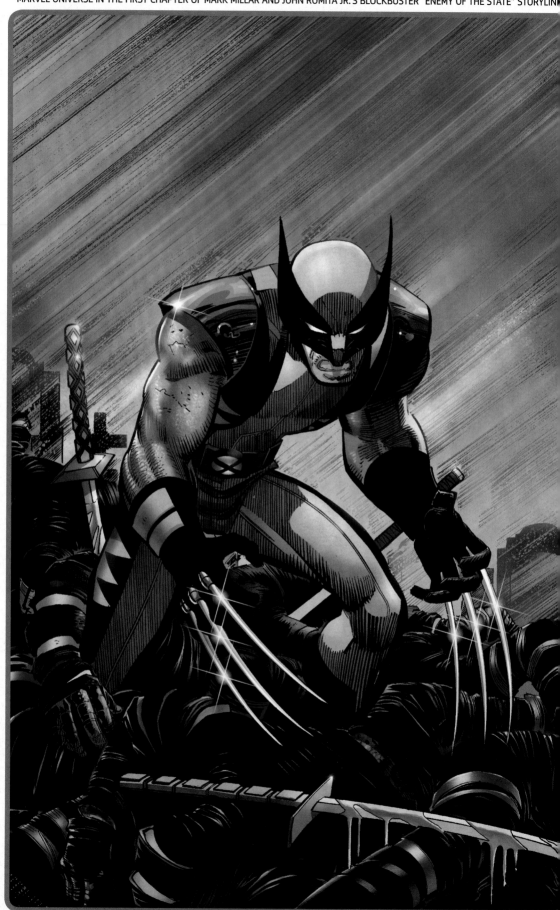

NAGASAKI, JAPAN.
OCTOBER

ICHIRO DROVE A BIG CAR, BUT HE WAS FAR FROM RICH. THE RICH GUY ALWAYS SAT IN THE BACK.

ICHIRO HAD BEEN HIS DRIVER FOR CLOSE TO FIFTEEN YEARS NOW, BUT HE WAS PRETTY SURE THE RICH GUY HADN'T SAID *FIFTEEN WORDS* TO HIM IN ALL THAT TIME.

HIS KID WAS GREAT, THOUGH. THE KID HAD HIS MOTHER'S EYES AND A HEARTY LAUGH AND PLAYED BASEBALL WITH ICHIRO'S BOY EVERY OTHER SATURDAY ON HIS WAY BACK FROM *MUSIC LESSONS.*

ICHIRO GOT A *KICK* OUT OF SEEING HOW LITTLE MONEY MATTERS WHEN YOU'RE TEN YEARS OLD. WHEN HAVING A BALL AND A BASEBALL MITT WAS ENOUGH TO MAKE TWO KIDS BEST FRIENDS FOR AN ENTIRE AFTERNOON.

LOOKING AT THEM RUN AND KICK AND SLIDE AND SHOUT, IT WAS IMPOSSIBLE TO TELL THEM APART SOMETIMES.

MAN, WHEN THEY WERE RUNNING WILD OUT THERE IN GREAT, BIG GLOVER PARK, EVEN *ICHIRO* SAID HE HAD TROUBLE TELLING THE RICH MAN'S KID FROM THE CHAUFFEUR'S SON.

UNFORTUNATELY, HE WASN'T THE *ONLY* ONE.

THE KIDNAPPERS WANTED TEN MILL IN U.S. DOLLARS. A LOT TO FIND EVEN IF HIS *OWN* BOY HAD BEEN SNATCHED, THE RICH MAN SAID, BUT FOR SOMEONE ELSE'S KID? WHAT COULD HE *DO* EXCEPT APOLOGIZE?

THE COPS WEREN'T MUCH USE EITHER. SURE, THEY TOOK SOME DETAILS, BUT THEY SPELLED HIS NAME WRONG THREE TIMES AND ICHIRO KNEW HE WASN'T WELL-HEELED ENOUGH TO KEEP THEM FOCUSED VERY LONG.

HOURS BECAME DAYS AND DAYS BECAME WEEKS.

AFTER A WHILE, THE COPS WOULDN'T EVEN TAKE HIS PHONE CALLS, AND ALL ICHIRO COULD THINK ABOUT WAS HOW DIFFERENT IT WOULD HAVE BEEN IF THE RICH MAN'S KID HAD BEEN BUNDLED INTO THAT CAR.

HIS SON HAD DISAPPEARED. *SNATCHED* IN *BROAD DAYLIGHT* AND, WHEN IT HIT THE NEWS, EVEN *THEY* JUST TALKED ABOUT THE RICH MAN.

I TOLD ICHIRO I WAS MAD HE DIDN'T CALL ME RIGHT AWAY.

ENEMY OF THE STATE
PART 1

| MARK MILLAR | JOHN ROMITA, JR. | KLAUS JANSON |
| WRITER | PENCILS & COVER | INKS |

| PAUL MOUNTS | VC'S RUS WOOTON | JENNIFER LEE |
| COLORS | LETTERS | EDITOR |

| AXEL ALONSO | JOE QUESADA | DAN BUCKLEY |
| EXECUTIVE EDITOR | EDITOR IN CHIEF | PUBLISHER |

SPECIAL THANKS TO *ERIC J. MOREELS*

I AIN'T AMERICAN. I'M A *CANADIAN*.

AMERICAN. CANADIAN. WHAT'S THE DIFFERENCE?

I ASSUME THAT IS OUR *MONEY* YOU HAVE IN THERE?

TEN MILLION BUCKS.

EXCELLENT. SUCH NONSENSE FROM YOUR BOSS THAT WE KIDNAPPED THE WRONG CHILD. WE ARE NOT STUPID.

WE KNEW THAT HE WAS ONLY TRYING TO GET HIS SON BACK CHEAP. ALL RICH MEN ARE THE SAME WHEN IT COMES TO MONEY.

...

IS THIS SUPPOSED TO BE *FUNNY*?

ACTUALLY, BACK HOME THAT'S SOMETHIN' OF AN *INSULT*.

AN *INSULT* HERE *TOO*, LITTLE MAN.

HEARTBEATS RACE. ADRENAL GLANDS KICK INTO OVERDRIVE. FEAR JUST *TRICKLES* FROM THEIR EVERY OPEN PORE...

THEY'RE DEAD BEFORE THEY HIT THE GROUND.

NO WAY.

SMELL AS DAMP AND AS MOLDY AS *EVERYTHING ELSE* SLEEPING UNDER THESE GRAVESTONES.

DIDN'T FEEL A *THING*.

YACHIMAE!

NO PULSE.

NO BREATH.

JOINTS SNAPPING AND POPPING WITH EVERY MOVE.

THESE THINGS HAVE BEEN DEAD FOR *AT LEAST* A MONTH.

OLD HAM GONE BAD ON A *HOT AFTERNOON*.

MOZZARELLA STENCH AT THE BACK OF MY *THROAT*.

IT'S A *SETUP*.

ICHIRO. THE KID.

FLYING HALFWAY AROUND THE WORLD IN *COACH* JUST TO SAVE A FEW BUCKS--

JACKASS PLAYING TETRIS--

CRACKING UP AT SOME BAD *ADAM SANDLER* FLICK--

--THE WHOLE WAY *HERE*.

I'LL SHOW 'EM WHERE THEY CAN STICK THEIR *TRAP*.

‹LOGAN IS OVERPOWERING THEM, MASTER. SHOULD WE STRIKE NOW BEFORE IT'S TOO LATE?›

‹NO, I WANT TO SEE WHAT THE WOLVERINE CAN DO. LET THEM TIRE HIM OUT A LITTLE.›

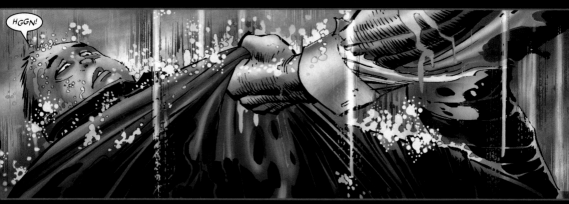

YOU KNOW, AS AN EX-ALTAR BOY OF SOME SEVEN YEARS STANDING, I FIND ALL THIS IMAGERY *VAGUELY* DISTURBING.

YEAH, BUT WE *DID* AND WHAT WE FOUND INSIDE WAS PRETTY *INTERESTING.* SMOKED OUT A PLOT TO TAKE DOWN CAPTAIN AMERICA, TONY STARK, CHARLIE XAVIER, REED RICHARDS...

ALL IN ALL, THEY WERE GOING FOR *SIXTEEN* KEY FIGURES IN THE SUPERHUMAN COMMUNITY. AND YOU KNOW WHO TOPPED THE LIST?

TELL ME.

MISTER WOLVERINE *HIMSELF.*

WELL, I GUESS THAT EXPLAINS WHAT *JAPAN* WAS ALL ABOUT. ANY IDEA WHO TOOK HIM DOWN? LOGAN'S NOT EXACTLY AN EASY MARK...

FROM WHAT WE'VE BEEN ABLE TO GATHER, THE ASSASSIN IN CHARGE OF THESE STRIKES CALLS HIMSELF *THE GORGON.*

APPARENTLY, HE'S A MUTANT FROM *KYOTO,* TAKEN DOWN BY THE LOCAL GANGS EIGHTEEN MONTHS AGO AND RESURRECTED BY *THE HAND* SOME THREE WEEKS LATER.

THINK YOU GOT TIME TO COME BACK AND HELP US OUT WITH THIS ONE?

FOR SOMETHING THIS BIG, I'LL *MAKE* THE TIME.

THIS SMELL AS BAD TO *YOU* AS IT DOES TO *ME*?

LIKE A *FART* IN AN ELEVATOR, ELEKTRA. LIKE A *FART* IN AN ELEVATOR.

COLONEL FURY? WE JUST GOT AN A-1 PRIORITY MESSAGE FROM INTERNATIONAL ALERTS. MISS NATCHIOS CLEARED FOR *ABOVE TOP SECRET?*

WHAT'S THE SITUATION, SOLDIER?

THEY JUST FOUND *WOLVERINE* IN *SOUTH AMERICA.*

--BURNED UP AND LYING IN A DITCH IN ARGENTINA. NO HAIR, ONE EYE, NINETY-PERCENT BURNS. GROUND-TEAM SAID HE LOOKED LIKE *HAMBURGER* MEAT.

WHAT ABOUT HIS *CAPTORS?* HOW DID HE *ESCAPE?*

DUNNO. *NOBODY KNOWS.* HIS BODY'S HEALING ITSELF DOWN IN *SICK BAY* RIGHT NOW, BUT HE HASN'T OPENED HIS EYES YET. WHATEVER THEY *DID* TO HIM BACK THERE EVEN HAD OUR *DOCTORS* HEAVING--

I GOTTA SAY, WOLVERINE, YOU'RE NOT LOOKING TOO GOOD, HONEY. THOSE *HYDRA* GUYS REALLY DID A *NUMBER* ON YOU, HUH?

ANTISEPTIC STINK. FOOTSTEPS SQUEAKING ON A HARD WAXED FLOOR. STARCHED LINEN SHEETS CHAFING MY--

HOSPITAL.

WHO *IS* THIS?

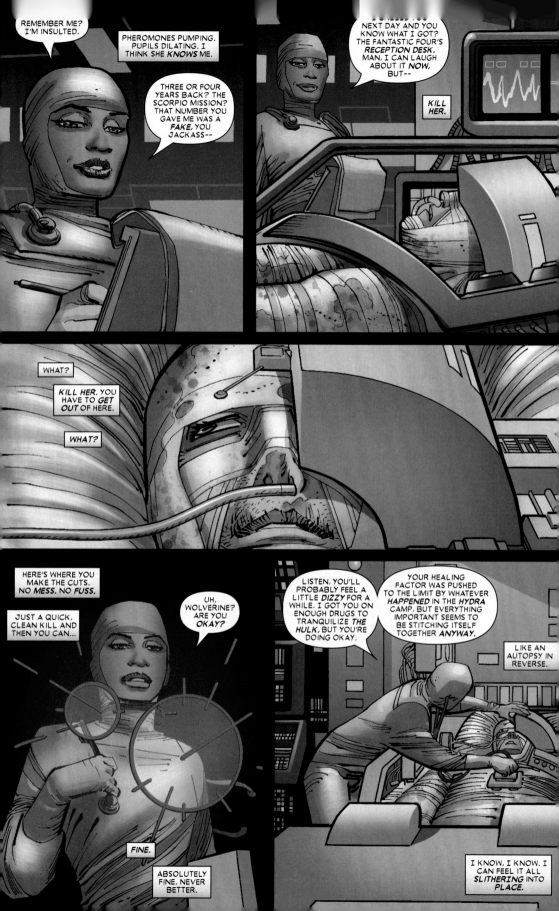

CONTINUED IN
WOLVERINE: ENEMY OF THE STATE
ULTIMATE COLLECTION TPB.

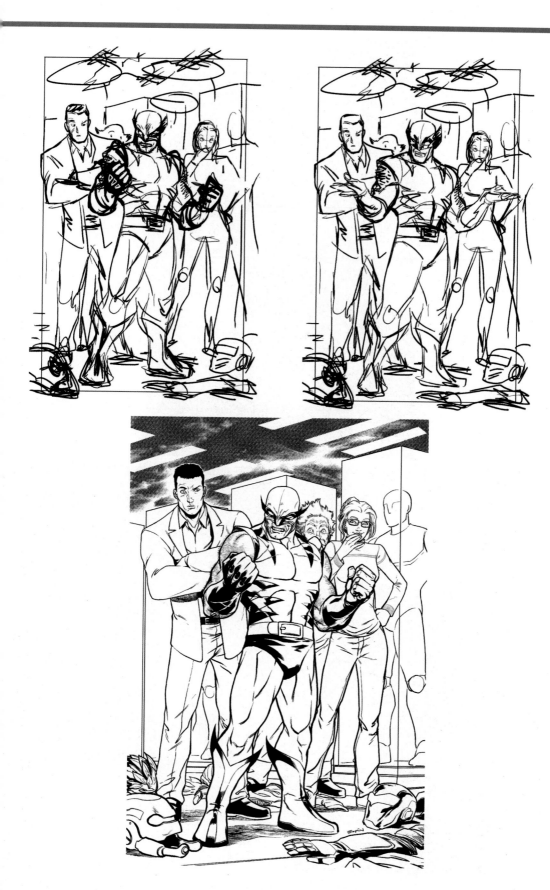

PAGE 51 LAYOUTS AND INKS

COVER SKETCHES BY JULIAN TOTINO TEDESCO